ABDO
Publishing Company

Skateboarding

MOVE YOUR BODY

A Kid's Guide to Fitness

A Buddy Book by **Sarah Tieck**

Buddy BOOKS
Move Your Body

VISIT US AT
www.abdopublishing.com

Published by ABDO Publishing Company, PO Box 398166, Minneapolis, MN 55439.

Copyright © 2013 by Abdo Consulting Group, Inc. International copyrights reserved in all countries. No part of this book may be reproduced in any form without written permission from the publisher. Buddy Books™ is a trademark and logo of ABDO Publishing Company.

Printed in the United States of America, North Mankato, Minnesota.
102012
012013

 PRINTED ON RECYCLED PAPER

Coordinating Series Editor: Rochelle Baltzer
Contributing Editors: Megan M. Gunderson, Marcia Zappa
Graphic Design: Jenny Christensen
Cover Photograph: *Shutterstock*: Vinicius Tupinamba.
Interior Photographs/Illustrations: *Eighth Street Studio* (p. 26); *Getty Images*: Zak Kendal (p. 21); *Glow Images*: ©Elmar Krenkel/Corbis (p. 25), ©Mike McGill/CORBIS (pp. 23, 29), ©Mika/Corbis (p. 17), Superstock (p. 11); *iStockphoto*: ©iStockphoto.com/ jordanchez (p. 9), ©iStockphoto.com/monkeybusinessimages (p. 27), ©iStockphoto.com/ skodonnell (p. 15), ©iStockphoto.com/THEGIFT777 (p. 5); *Photo Researchers, Inc.*: 3D4Medical (p. 13); *Shutterstock*: nito (p. 19), ostill (p. 30); *Thinkstock*: FogStock (p. 7), Hemera (p. 7), iStockphoto (p. 30), Stockbyte (p. 13), Thinkstock Images (p. 23).

Library of Congress Cataloging-in-Publication Data

Tieck, Sarah, 1976-
  Skateboarding / Sarah Tieck.
    p. cm. -- (Move your body: a kid's guide to fitness)
  ISBN 978-1-61783-563-6 (hardcover)
1. Skateboarding--Juvenile literature. I. Title.
  GV859.8.T54 2013
  796.22--dc23
                    2012032932

Table of Contents

Healthy Living

Your body is amazing! A healthy body helps you feel good and live well. In order to be healthy, you must take care of yourself. One way to do this is to move your body.

Regular movement gives you **energy** and makes you stronger. Many kinds of exercise can help you do this. One fun type of exercise is skateboarding! Let's learn more about skateboarding.

Children should get 60 minutes of movement every day. Skateboarding is a great way to do this!

Skateboarding 101

Skateboarders move their bodies on skateboards. They place their feet on the board. They use their legs to push off and direct their movement. Their arm, abdominal, and back muscles help them balance and do moves!

People skateboard in driveways, on sidewalks, on trails, or at skate parks. You can skateboard for hours or just a few minutes. And, you can choose moves that are easy or hard!

Skateboarding moves require balance and skill.

It is important to learn how to ride and stop before trying more challenging moves.

Skateboarding movements are called tricks. People invent new ones all the time! The ollie is a basic trick. Once you learn it, you can learn others more easily.

In an ollie, the back end of the board is kicked down. Then, the skateboarder jumps up.

Let's Get Physical

People exercise to stay fit. Regular exercise makes you more flexible. It helps you stay at a healthy body weight. It can also help prevent health problems later in life.

Skateboarding can be a type of aerobic exercise. It makes your lungs and heart work hard to get your body more oxygen. The more often you skateboard, the easier it will be to breathe and move.

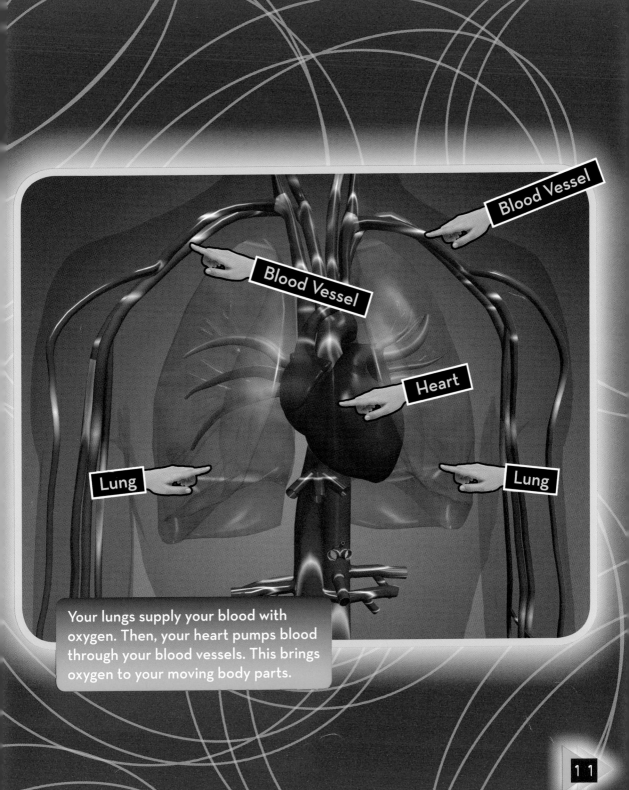

Blood Vessel

Blood Vessel

Heart

Lung

Lung

Your lungs supply your blood with oxygen. Then, your heart pumps blood through your blood vessels. This brings oxygen to your moving body parts.

Skateboarding also builds your **muscles**. When you do jumps and turns, you work your leg muscles. Some tricks use your arms and shoulders. And, your **abdominal** and back muscles help you balance.

Over time, your muscles will get stronger. Then you'll be able to do tricks more easily!

WORD OF MOUTH

Skateboarding makes your bones stronger.

Your leg muscles help you push off and move on your skateboard.

Quadriceps

Hamstring Muscles

Calf Muscle

Gearing Up

All skateboarders need a skateboard. This is a strong piece of specially shaped wood. It has four wheels underneath. These allow it to turn and move.

Skateboarders should always wear a helmet. It is a good idea to also wear knee pads, wrist guards, elbow pads, and gloves.

Skateboarders wear comfortable clothing. They also wear sneakers to help them hold onto the skateboard.

WORD OF MOUTH

Some skateboarders dress for style as well as movement.

When you put on your helmet, fasten the straps. Make sure the helmet is tight enough to stay in place. If it isn't on correctly, it won't help you!

Play It Safe

Every year, many kids are hurt in skateboarding accidents. Skateboarders can get badly hurt from a fall. Some even have to go to the hospital. So, it is important to be careful when you skateboard.

If you fall off your skateboard, be sure to check for injuries. And if you hit your head, you should replace your helmet.

The best way to stay safe is to wear a helmet specially made for skateboarding. Wear pads to guard your skin and bones. And, start out on a smooth, flat surface.

When you learn new tricks, pay attention to how you feel. If you are tired, don't push yourself. You are more likely to get hurt when your body is tired. And if you are learning, go slowly.

For safety, avoid skateboarding in the rain or in wet areas. Water can also harm your skateboard.

WORD OF MOUTH

One way to stay safe is to join a skate club. There, others can help you learn new tricks. You can also take skateboarding lessons.

Ready? Set? Go!

Skateboarders need to be flexible. Taking time to stretch can help with this. Over time, stretching makes it easier for your body to move.

Before you stretch, warm up by walking or doing other easy movement. This loosens your muscles so you can stretch better.

After skateboarding, cool down by walking and stretching. Cooling down helps keep your muscles from getting sore.

Warming up and stretching prepares your muscles to work hard during exercise.

WORD OF MOUTH

Don't wear headphones while you skateboard. They make it hard to hear what is going on around you.

Look and Learn

When you are skateboarding, be aware of your surroundings. At a skate park, go slowly until you are comfortable with a move. If the park has an area for beginners, stay there while you learn. And, always watch for others.

Skateboarding can be **challenging**, even on a driveway or a sidewalk. You need to watch for cars, bikes, and people. Also watch for cracks in pavement or objects in your path.

Skateboarders must pay attention to hills and turns on paths and at skate parks.

Take Care

Grip tape covers a skateboard's wooden board, or deck. It helps the skateboarder keep from slipping. Sometimes decks break or grip tape wears away. So, check your skateboard's deck, gears, and wheels before you use it.

Many skateboarders also wear special shoes. They look like sneakers, but they are made to hold up to skateboarding. Over time, they get worn from doing tricks. So be sure your shoes are in good condition.

Brain Food

How do you know if skateboarding is enough of a workout?

Some people just pay attention to how their bodies feel. Others measure their heart rate. This is the number of times your heart beats per minute.

A tool called a heart rate monitor measures this. You can also find this on your own by counting heartbeats. Touch the inside of your wrist or the side of your neck. Then, count the pulses you feel in one minute.

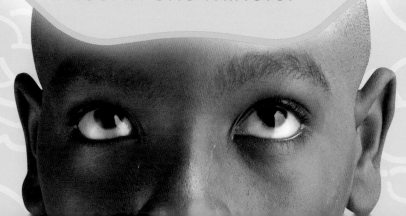

What is the best food to eat for skateboarding?

You need lots of energy to skateboard. So, eat food from all of the food groups. Carbohydrates from grains or fresh fruit give you energy. Meats, seafood, beans, eggs, and nuts help your body build bones and muscles.

Are there different skateboards for kids?

Skateboarders of all ages and sizes can use the same size boards. Skateboards come in many different styles. And, there are different quality skateboards. For your safety, choose one that is good quality.

Choose to Move

Remember that skateboarding is a type of fitness that makes your body stronger. Fitness is an important part of a healthy life. Skateboard as often as you can. Each positive choice you make will help you stay healthy.

Skateboarding is an activity you can do alone or with friends.

HEALTHY BODY FILES

FEEL GOOD

✔ Water plays an important part in helping your body build **muscle**. So, be sure to drink some before, during, and after skateboarding.

✔ Falling is part of skateboarding. To soften your fall, try to land on your bottom instead of your hands, elbows, or knees.

PLAY NICE

✔ Use your manners at a skate park. Take turns and be friendly to others.

✔ Watch out for other skateboarders. You can be hurt if you hit each other.

TAKE CARE

✔ You can get sweaty and dirty while skateboarding. Take a bath or shower to clean up afterward!

✔ Skateboarders are usually outside. Wear sunscreen to avoid sunburning your skin.

Important Words

abdominal relating to the part of the body between the chest and the hips.

aerobic (ehr-OH-bihk) relating to exercise that increases oxygen in the body and makes the heart better able to use oxygen.

carbohydrate (kahr-boh-HEYE-drayt) a food source that includes sugars and starches. Fruit, bread, pasta, and sweets have a lot of carbohydrates.

challenging (CHA-luhn-jihng) testing one's strengths or abilities.

energy (EH-nuhr-jee) the power or ability to do things.

flexible able to bend or move easily.

lungs body parts that help the body breathe.

muscle (MUH-suhl) body tissue, or layers of cells, that helps move the body.

oxygen (AHK-sih-juhn) a colorless gas that humans and animals need to breathe.

Web Sites

To learn more about skateboarding, visit ABDO Publishing Company online. Web sites about skateboarding are featured on our Book Links page. These links are routinely monitored and updated to provide the most current information available.

www.abdopublishing.com

Index